About the Author

Daphne Denley is a poet and song-writer. This is her first published collection of poetry. She lives on the edge of Rodborough Common with her husband and daughter.

Moments

Daphne Denley

Crumps Barn Studio

*For my loving husband Ben and beautiful
daughter Felicity, who make my life complete*

Crumps Barn Studio LLP
Crumps Barn, Syde, Cheltenham GL53 9PN
www.crumpsbarnstudio.co.uk

Copyright © Daphne Denley 2019
First printed 2019

The right of Daphne Denley to be identified as the author of this work has been asserted by her in accordance with the Copyright, Designs and Patents Act 1988.

All rights reserved. No part of this publication may be reproduced, stored in a retrieval system, or transmitted in any form or by any means, electronic, mechanical, photocopying, recording or otherwise, without the prior permission of the copyright owner.

Cover image: 'Moments' mixed media on board by Jeremy Brookes 2019

ISBN 978-1-9998705-6-0

Dear Reader,

Life throws everyone challenges, but it is also fascinating when you take the time to evaluate your feelings, experiences, people and everything around you.

I'm a fully signed-up apprentice of mid-life mayhem. Constantly trying to work out what I should be doing, at my age and time of life.

Three years ago, my husband and I, with our daughter of six, a typical family unit, went about our daily life and routine. Every day, similar as the last, happy enough, but without truly appreciating what we had.

Disaster then struck, as the older we've got, the inevitable problems began. My husband became seriously ill – it was bowel cancer. The time that followed included an emergency operation and six months of intensive chemotherapy.

Our lives were turned upside down, but especially for our daughter. So young to have to deal with such difficult times and emotions. Not old enough to possibly comprehend it all.

As wife and mum, I felt the need to regain my positivity and strength for all of us. To try not show any weakness, or allow this to beat us.

Routine was my key plan. Work, school, and carrying on about our daily lives as normally as possible became a must.

Unfortunately, there is no guide book on how you should cope in these situations, as everyone faces different scenarios and difficulties.

However, I started to reflect on life and actually live each day for what it was, but also wanted to get back in touch with who I am.

I began writing things down, as a way to vent some emotions. This became the ultimate therapy for me.

As a singer in local bands in my spare time, I am happy with rhyme. As a young lady, I always fancied myself as a bit of a song writer, so poetry feels a natural way of writing.

My poems aren't all about our situation, but things I've seen and subjects that are possibly difficult for people to broach.

I remembered past issues, but also started to appreciate and document other people, nature and the world around me.

In my emotional state, the words kept flowing. Ideas came at all times of the day and night.

Writing was also a great tool to escape the day. For quiet time, reflection, gathering thoughts and clearing my mind. So I could hopefully face whatever confronted us.

Since then, my husband has continued to battle, with two further cancerous lumps being removed from his liver.

However, this aside, as well as some on-going trials, as a family, we still remain strong. What started being self-help, writing has now become a bit of an addiction.

I hope that these poems help you to tap into your emotions and question your thoughts. Maybe you become engrossed, so escape into a quiet space for a while.

You may find similarities in your own life, situations and feelings. This then act as a catalyst, in helping you to realise those times to cherish, or the need to rectify things in the future.

It is my mission to be thankful and mindful of everything and everyone around me, as life is too short. So, thank you for taking your time to read my book of poems.

May these 'Moments', captured in time, enrich your life, as they've helped mine.

Daphne Denley

Contents

Sweet Dreams – 3

Precious Time – 4

Rat Race – 5

Cards Apart – 6

Past, Present, Future – 7

Cat of Greed – 8

Bully – 9

Baby, Girl, Lady, Me – 10

Fit Club Fun – 11

Are We Alive? – 12

Accused – 13

Stressed – 14

Afternoon Sky – 16

Beautiful, But Deadly – 17

October's Breath – 18

Class Below – 19

Cluttered Be – 20

Committed – 21

Numbing News – 22

Head Space – 23

Dispute – 24

Morning Routine – 25

Weeds In Life – 27

Daydreaming Prey – 28

My Era – 30

On The Edge – 31

Oh Baby – 32

Troubled Times – 34

Desperate – 36

Inevitable – 37

Night Fear – 38

Slippery Slope – 39

Heart Ache – 40

Treasured Friends – 41

Just Pretend – 43

Brain Retrain – 44

Misery – 45

The Customer Service Call – 46

They're Wrong, You're Right! – 47

Addiction – 48

So, We Meet – 49

Apple! – 50

Born Organiser – 51

This Year's End – 52

So Where Was I? – 53

What's That Smell? – 54

Treat – 55

Is – 56

New Lease of Life – 57

Springtime's Arrived – 59

Friday Nights – 60

Conveniences Etiquette – 61

Equality? – 62

Express Your Voice – 63

Cheers – 64

Moments

Sweet Dreams

Gently breathing, sleeping sound
Cuddled up and curled around
Fantasy dreaming, excitement now
As little twitches, noises aloud
So, I watch, and really wonder
What magical place, or spell you're under
Let me in, I'd love to share
Must hug you now, as do so care
Comfort, warmth and love from mother
But careful, not awake the slumber

Precious Time

So scared each day that passes by
One less chance to savour life

What happened today, that will remind
A memory to treasure, or moment in time

As older we get, days, weeks and months
The years they merge, together clumped

What age am I, and how long do I have
Before no longer walk this mortal path

Cling tight to those loved young and old
Together stories create, future to unfold

Rat Race

Try tick all boxes, am disorganised mess
Forever chasing, where to go next
House chores are stacking, as pushed aside
Convenience eating, to claw back time

More important, socialise and drink
Than respect myself, or stop to think
The diary is so full of things
Dread turn the page, what next it brings

A Groundhog Day, lifestyle a trial
No way it seems to break the cycle
A challenge now as need to change
Or self-destruct, in this rat race

Cards Apart

A card each Birthday and Christmas write
Yet seldom meet, as short of time

When sat alone, do sometimes ponder
Why different paths, apart we wondered

Duty bound, always polite
Keep pretence, considered right

Truth be known, we'd rather leave
The past behind, just memories keep

Good times we had, but that was then
Our future plans, together end

Continue to think, meet up we might
But actually know we'll only write

Past, Present, Future

Watching seasons, come and go
Holidays, birthdays, quickly flow
Halt a minute and stop the clock
Or you will find life's memories lost
Try planning things for every day
Capture your history, so can relay
As we get older, time moves fast
Embrace the future, as beloved past

Cat of Greed

Always hungry, with loving stares
My cat Bumble meows in despair

If allowed, he'd eat and eat
And only stop when needing sleep

His belly would rub along the floor
Then struggle moving, legs and paws

Luckily, isn't a good mouser
Just begs around our legs and trousers

So crazy when the morning comes
Loud meows and purrs 'til we get up

When we're eating, glares at us
Rolls onto back, and makes a fuss

We love him, even though a pest
Part of our family, happiness

As long as we don't over feed
Long time we'll have our cat of greed

Bully

Green eyed monster in my class
Always mean, wishes me last

Dirty stares, boo's, points and laughs
Calling names, sneer as I pass

Tells lies, fooling most my friends
On best behaviour, she pretends

It's her, she cries, to clear her name
I mostly end up taking blame

Bully born from broken love
Hurt vented on unlucky some

In time she'll learn, cruelty don't pay
As loneliness, it brings your way

Victim she is, but inflicts pain
Jealous it's clear, so full of hate

Baby, Girl, Lady, Me

She's growing up, can't stop this no
But wish her young, as precious so

Innocence still, as sleeps at night
When tucked up, cuddling teddy tight

Scared to lose, out on today
Our memories, must not fade away

Time moves fast, so hope with that
Always treasures, her lifetime past

So proud, she has such future dreams
And even more, as just like me

Fit Club Fun

Cartwheel, handstand, roll and fly
Bounce, somersault, flip so high
Flossing, spins, jump to the sky
To name a few my girl will try

Dancing, swimming, trampolining
Gymnastics clubs, all so exhausting
Football, sewing, athletics and tennis
I'm losing track of what she's best

As I sit here, while she's a clubbing
A needed rest from taxi mumming
So tired I am, it's nice to doze
Until it's time, next episode

So she is fit, and that besides
Better life has she, to date than mine
And friends a plenty, she gathers up
Great start in life, and so much fun

Are We Alive?

Am I here, and what is real?
Is this dream? Imagined spiel?
What I touch, smell and feel
Did I really taste this meal?

What if life is just pretend
Together think, it starts and ends
A lottery too, with whom you share
The living memories, love and care

In the morning do we wake
Or do subconscious thoughts create
Out of body, our mind it makes
A story that is really fake

Ever dreamt you woke inside?
But asleep you were, still in the night
Our brains so clever, can't deny
The possibility, your life's a lie

Accused

It wasn't me, yet somehow I'm blamed
Too easy a target as never do hate

What devious person to so turn around
Apparently, I said, but mouth didn't sprout

My words against theirs, no evidence found
Crocodile tears, always seem to win out

So punished again, a victim in spite
As labelled the bully, and couldn't be right

Stressed

Do you ever feel in life, that stress has taken over?
And if you dare to think too much, you wouldn't
    cope much longer?
Acceptance there's a problem, messes with your
    mind and breathing
As try to stop the thoughts inside, and hide from
    your true feelings

Shake of head, force reaction, try to run away
Think of places you can hide and keep worries at bay
Way too busy every day, so need to write things
    down
But such a mess and still forget, just going around
    and round

It's got so bad, you dread the sound, phone message
    has arrived
Or bumping into folk you know, avoid to catch their
    eye
Heart beats hard within your chest, with twinges in
    your veins
Shaking sometimes, shortened breath, and random
    body pain

Even if are resting, in the quietest place can find
Still full of angst and can't relax or put troubles aside
The answer may come soon enough, when body says
    it's time
And rush no more, you'll have no choice, as
    grounded with a sign

Afternoon Sky

I stare to the sky, and escape in the clouds
Shapes make pictures, time changes around

Colours some vibrant, that whirl and blend
With tracks from airplanes, sweeping lines like pen

I try to paint, and capture in film
But nothing compares, to seeing for real

Earth's global pallet, so far from the land
Pray not be ruined, by a human hand

Beautiful, But Deadly

Rivers of the sky, water the land, cleaning Earth's own
Yet rivers of the soul, sink deep, leak when overflow
Burning of the sun, help the flowers and trees to show
Yet burning of the skin, scars and makes cancer grow
Whispers in the wind, blows dust and cobwebs away
Yet whispers unkind, blows your mind astray
Fires rage, cull un-want, give light and warmth
Yet fires destroy, the heart, the mind left torched
Natures force, beautiful, but deadly
If lessons unlearnt
Then consequences plenty

October's Breath

Sudden breeze across my face
Alerted senses, try to trace
Hairs stood up on arms and back
Body shivers, shock attack
Scared to turn my head around
Ears are listening for a sound
Eyes so wide, lids cold inside
Totally still and petrified
Finally moving from the space
Nothing, no-one in this place
Something strange has caused this fear
Eerie, silent atmosphere
Thoughts of strangers in my head
Ghosts from the past, now long time dead
As closer, Halloween draws near
What lurks about the air unclear
Wind it whistles, sometimes roars
Blowing gusts and slamming doors
Orange skies, leaves and pumpkins
Colder nights and darker mornings
Spider webs catch all that pass
Evening skies, of owls and bats
Blanket mist and fog descends
Persistent rain and frosts begin
Autumn's here and Summer's left
Welcomed in October's breath

Class Below

Something on the sole of shoe
Is how I feel, because of you

Non response, or little words
Sudden cold, now feelings hurt

Below the grade where you exist
Your perception no longer fit

How naive of you to think
I stand below and must not mix

Come crashing down, you surely will
If you now lose the friendships built

No one likes self-righteous fools
And loneliness can be so cruel

For you hereon, I do now pray
That you can change your selfish ways

Or on your own, create your fate
And hard for me, but friendship break

Cluttered Be

Embarrassed I have no time to spend
On house and garden maintenance

Every room, is in a muddle
Too much around, you could call rubble

When friends and family come here to visit
Apologise for all the messes in it

In my mind, I have a plan
To sort the house, and ground around

But feel it's far too hard to reach
An ambition, only I will seek

Extensions, skips, tidy garage and shed
Stay fiction, really, in my head

Miracles might happen, house fire, money win
Then move away, to start again

It's hard to think of another way now
I must buck up, pull finger out

Committed

Shivers about my body
Clammy hands and brow
Don't believe I'm really here
Not sure if should get out
Looking over shoulder
Could I run away
Was this a bad decision
Stupidity or brave
Squirming as am waiting
For the start of what's to come
It's too late, as heart does race
Committed I've become

Numbing News

Numbed up feelings, as just can't think straight
Mind actively blocking, emotional strains
Actually sober, but dizzy in ways
Drifting off driving, expression is dazed
Tired, exhausted, shouldn't still work
But have to keep going, and push though it hurts
More saying sorry, and covering the facts
Errors, mistakes, show through the cracks
Eyes hot and heavy, they sting in the light
As holding back tears, an on-going fight
Headaches within, only pills can subside
Allowing your poison to own you at night
The news you'd been dreading is finally told
Reality sucks, and the worst leaves you cold
Shocked by the truth, though deep down you knew
That glimmer of maybe, now cut down in two
Here we go again, goes around in your head
Memories of last time, "do I have the strength"?
So battle on you must, and get tough once again
As fear that it's beaten you, and this is the end.

Head Space

In another world and drifting away
From the hustle and bustle surrounding my day

Subconsciously carry on with working on tasks
In automatic pilot, no worries may crash

Now as I imagine a real special place
Somewhere when dreaming, I love to escape

Beach, mountain lodge, clearing deep in the woods
Not paying attention as I really should

Then break through the silence, a very loud bang
Out of day dreams, right back here and now

Maybe I should not let mind wander off
But feel so much better in fantasies lost

Dispute

Evaporation of the steam around your head
Exploding anger, abuse and insults that are said

Condensation forms, and tears run down my face
Drops of water, now black mascara stained

Heated exchange, as the sweat turns into blood
Hearts are racing, shocked that violence had been done

Then silence, as the only sound is breath
Sighs as sharing, looks and hugs of sad regret

Morning Routine

Muddled mum is at it again
Her mood, well frankly, it's insane
She lost her keys, and got quite frantic
Up and down the stairs in panic
Eventual relief when at last found
Not in the door, but on the ground
Now there she is, off shouting loud
"Put your shoes on", running around
"We do this every single day,
But never manage quick away"
Sometimes I feel that she should chill
Or mummy will just become ill
"I'm doing it now", I scream again
Then realise oops, the look of dread
Here it comes, I tightly brace
"It's your fault dear, if you are late"
Army fashion, I'm strapped with coat
School bag on back, then told to halt
"Did I lock the door, and windows bolt?"
Five more minutes while she scampers
In and out, now moving faster
"Ok let's go" at last she ponders
"Come on mum, I'll miss the register"
Finally, we are out the gate
Now run to school, that bit I hate
Think this is bad, well half I've told
We've pets to feed, and lunch to fold

Let alone the routine wake
With dressing, teeth and washing face
After getting me out of my dreams
So mad is mum, and hard it seems
But love each other, we didn't mean
It's just our typical Morning Routine!

Weeds In Life

Like the weeds in the garden, stifling as become strong
That weave in and grow upon, stealing water and sun
Without those below them, they'd struggle to crop
Their roots would lie dormant, dried up and forgot
The strength they have gained is from other plants' lead
Support and foundations, when huddled between
The weed is then greedy and has to move on
Only to find that its time in life's gone
The fighters below, still alive holding on
Even though they were bullied, are clearly most strong
What lengths would you go to for personal gain?
Do you step on others and cause undue pain?
Are you taking credit for things didn't do?
Forgetting without them, there's nothing to you
Don't relish in glory as you're moving on
Yes, soon to be history, as weeds don't belong

Daydreaming Prey

Precious time evaporates, as daydreams envelop your thinking space.

Beams of light flicker as you daze, mind is elsewhere consumed in gaze.

Eyes are cold, fixed staring glazed, body frozen still and straight.

Voices muddled words blocked out, just random noise and sounds around.

A gush of air your head awakes, turn of head and body shakes.

Confused a second while you try, remember who, what, where am I.

Sinking deep within your chair, looking around to see who's there.

Did they see you unaware, and catch you drift without a care?

Life demands full concentration, on the job, must pay attention.

Beware subconscious could remain, daydream or reality tricks your brain.

My Era

Big hair, been long time like that
An icon, of happy times past
Not wanting, to grow up inside
So, cling on, to youth with this style
As others, may jeer, criticise
Attention, being different, the prize
The look that, one era had found
Someday, will sure come back around

On The Edge

Imagine stabbing your thoughts away
As constantly in your mind they plague
A quiet moment to reflect
Is full of dread and hard regrets
Shake your head, chant it's ok
But never deal with, or erase
So back the thoughts, they come again
Mind stab them, deeply breathing in
So scared to face, it builds within
More stress and worry, anger and sin
Danger that those thoughts you fledge
Will push you now, over the edge
And burst all banks, in crazy rants
Unleashed the dark and twisted angst

Oh Baby

Oh Baby, finding hard the words to say,
How sorry, that it has to be this way.
Scared for you, know that you feel the same,
Uncertain, of how many days remain.

Oh Baby, don't ever think it was in vain,
Your struggle, all the unbelievable pain.
A fighter, facing fears, denying change,
The wish tomorrow, turns into better days.

Oh Baby, helped so many in your time,
Hope, care and loving, to everyone beside.
Kindest heart, and arms so open wide,
Did your best, and what believed was right.

Oh Baby, glad we met along the way,
A friend I call you, sharing memories we made.
If time allowed, would do everything again,
As without you, life beyond won't be the same.

Oh Baby, don't be sad and don't you cry,
Carry real pride, for every avenue you tried.
I wish that, all of your dreams will carry on,
Forever lasting, even after you are gone.

Oh Baby, this is not your last goodbye,
Within us, your light will still shine bright.
And remember, only briefly leave our side,
As together, one day, we'll join you in the sky.

Troubled Times

Sometimes by day, you block the fears
And shake away the thoughts and tears
Must keep going, ignore the pain
Be stronger, chants within your brain
I'm alright, you lie to others
Convince yourself, keep undercover
But within the cracks are forming
Jolting twitch, a violent warning
Sudden breath, stood to attention
Facing up to realisation
Run and hide, your instinct says
Like vulnerable child, in many ways
Eyes they well, stare hard to stop
As weakness shown, is a big not
So, through the days, while things are bad
Must keep your cool and not be sad
By night you shuffle and sweat in fright
As day's events, brought back to life
Re-living every second played
A torture no one can erase
So, in your dreams you have to fight
Try waking up, though asleep tight
Shouting out, your heart in race
Gasp in relief, at last awake

Such worry now, this has become
Pray for yourself, and everyone
Keep telling yourself that you are fine
Even though you are
In troubled times

Desperate

Desperate to hear good news, but diagnosis down

Desperate for remedy, to turn this all around

Desperate as hanging on the doctor's every word

Desperate as the surgeon works to rectify the hurt

Desperate now to see you soon, as need to hold you tight

Desperate you will get through this, be once again alright

Desperate for all that this nightmare is soon over

Desperate that desperate goes, and desperate no longer

Inevitable

It's a case of when, rather than if
As no body is immune to this
Ignorance surely can be bliss
But to hide away poses more risk

Night Fear

Alien sounds came in the night
That made me hold the covers tight
Absolutely still, breathing slight
Intently listening, for familiar cries
Really hope this can't hear me
Frightened attract what I don't see
Gradually peeling sheets away
Twist my body and legs astray
Curtains giving way to lights
Curiosity gripped with what I find
Suddenly bang, the lights go out
Deathly silence, I stop in fright
Feel the floor under my feet
Holding breath, scared of repeat
One minute passes, feels least five
Slowly forward, take a stride
Arm in front, grab curtains tight
Tentatively looking up to find
Nothing, but the dark outside
So sleeping now, half open eyes

Slippery Slope

Killing me quicker than I really should
Abusing my body, so not treating good
Ignoring reality, deluding myself
Actions I'm taking destroying my health
Evidence showing with lines on my face
Stomach is churning, and body it aches
Yawn in my coffee, take vitamins vile
So try counteract, my demise denial
Poisoned within, yet still keep on going
Torturous harm, the damage unknowing
Should I continue, then would it be fate
As caught in this cycle, is it now too late?
The mornings of pain, regrets a plenty
Become too frequent, once few, now many
Scared to question, why this is so wrong
Must change soon, 'fore my time has gone.

Heart Ache

Your heart aches as you imagine the pain
The worry they have and troubles now face

Take it away, you would if you could
Relieving troubles, to try making good

Yet desperate struggles still fight every day
Deny the inevitable, refuse to go this way

The strength in their love, is all that is left
As medicine fails, though doctors did best

Family and friends, are helpless it seems
But memories forged, forever in dreams

Time a great healer, but never forget
Life so full of heartache, 'til cruellest death

Treasured Friends

Remember the days, when was bullied at school
Went home most days crying, and branded a fool
Asked why am I different, what do I do wrong?
As just don't belong here, fit in with no one

Mum wrapped arms around me, said it was ok
Someday you will fit in, things will go your way
You know that I love you, that's all you should know
So no longer worry, with your heart of gold ... You'll
    find friends

Then one day I noticed, it wasn't just me
Another soul crying, who looked so lonely
I offered my ear, listened on intently
You soon will be happy, things aren't as they seem

My arm wrapped around them, said it is ok
Let me help you fix it, so things go your way
I want to be there, that's all you should know
Please trust me this one time, your worries will go ...
    I'm your friend

So, in the dark times, when I feel alone
Think friends that I have, are those that we sewn
Through love of each other, not ones that were forced
But people connections, and truly engrossed

Each one whom I know, will always so care
As so I do trust, forever be there
Each wrap arms around us, we say it's ok
Together we do this, keep trouble at bay

We know that the love, unspoken is there
And every heartbeat, is flooding with care ...
      Love my friends xx

Just Pretend

Be someone else, sometimes we try
Dressing up to trick the eye

Carefully planned to the last detail
Imagination, ideas and stories of people

Escape from one's own trials in life
And live as another, act in disguise

To be so special, you really dream
One day, someone might dress as me

In fantasy now, true to the role
Further, into character involved

In a second, you had forgot
Person dressed as, you are not

Brain Retrain

With space, allow thoughts to escape
Or rethread, so fall back in place

Mixed directions, just can't process
Or understand, the which way is best

Roll of the dice, roulette defined
Decision blindly, did decide

As vacant minds, need to align
Cleanse the empty, renew the files

If by chance, time gifted with
Retrain the Brain, as head must fix

Misery

What do you say, it is that bad
Avoid the silence, so idle chat
The tears they roll, eyes puffy red
Hanky sodden, snuffled in breath
Heart has been ripped, it's very sad
The cruellest blow, this soul has had
Just want to fix, the problem now
But nothing will, there's no way how
Love, hugs and food, the only vaccine
Before the time, will surely remedy
It's hard to think, this hardship pass
Have faith, that misery, seldom last

The Customer Service Call

Customer service, hmm that's what it's called
But is a poor someone, a barrier, the wall
Who has to apologise, but told not agree
The way business shafts us, yet show sympathy
Sorry again, but the computer says no
I have procedures, that we must follow
Avoiding the questions, going quiet at times
So very unhelpful, your patience now tried
Recording your call, as you get angry
For training they say, but evidence see
Now black on your record, as you fight your case
They'll claw back for legal, your privacy traced
Still no further forward, all exhausted, no fun
Was waste of a phone call, just business that won
The survey then follows, just how did we do
After highly raised voices, surely, they knew?

They're Wrong, You're Right!

It's not selfish to allow your feelings out,
If you always think of others, in the main, before
    yourself.

It's not wrong to allow, being spoilt from time to time,
As you rarely see the money, you've worked so hard to
    find.

Don't need to justify, going out for that wild night,
And constantly stress or worry, what others think of
    your life.

Be proud of being you, as no other can be like,
Strive to stay an individual, not belittled, always fight.

Feel ashamed and paranoid, while people appear to
    always whisper?
A little jealous they could be, wish they had your life
    elixir.

Celebrate in always knowing, a happy road you lead in
    spite
Shout it out, if in doubt, rest assured, They're Wrong,
    You're Right!

Addiction

Shaking hands, missing heart beats, gasping, shortened breath
As quickly grabbing, fast indulging, in forbidden bets.
Blocking out the reasons, and the thoughts that this is wrong
As the prize is far too wanted, and desperately longed.

Then panic sets in for a while, as you shake your head
As in the moment realise, you did it once again.
The guilt you feel and disbelief, that weakness you possess
And fear you've lost your self-control, and only answer yes.

Too late to go back, change the past, as now what's done is done.
Just have to live with consequence, and face the web you've spun.
The next time you'll be stronger, so you tell yourself again.
Must combat your addiction, not fuel with more regrets.

So, We Meet

Smiles from a stranger, who could then become a friend
You look and wonder, if your lives together blend
So, walk closer, move towards each other's space
In the moment, block surroundings, eyes fixate
A first hello, tensions broke, welcomed relief
With nervous giggles, in between the words we speak
Holding on now as realise it's time to part
Anticipation, that a new relation starts

Apple!

From bag to box, between I'm tossed
A promise be eaten, so quickly lost
Three days now I have changed my place
But no one tempted to eat my face
Not covered in shiny paper or bag
No words across my chest to brag
But goodness inside, you would unlock
If teeth sink in, and jaws did want
Beige food and stodge, so do continue
And fat it gathers, outside and in you
Hunger temporarily subsides
Nutritional needs, you didn't find
Oh, nag they do, to eat your fruit
Yes, you need me, I'm good for you
New life from me, tree could have grown
If dropped on ground, and seed had sewn
So, health you neglect, good intentions lost
Then I grew for nothing, and so too will rot

Born Organiser

So, they say, it's in my blood
My star sign says I am the one

But seriously now, it stresses me out
My muddled head is in self doubt

And though I dread, I face the fear
As no one else will volunteer

For a good cause it always is
Some funds are raised, and many win

Pulling together those who do struggle
Communicating, with each other

Finally, yes, the deed is done
As really wasn't that much fun

Pain it is, a labour of love
But organise savvy, I've become

This Year's End

So full of drama, indecision and disaster
Story book of horrors, nervous laughter
Trials at times, impossible to face
Wanting out, this awful place
Yet sometimes, overwhelming joy
Relief, smiles, comfort and warmth
Love from family, friends and strangers
Restoring faith and hopes, my saviour
Now as this year, comes to an end
Mixed feelings, parting kisses send
To wish for a better year, I could
But instead, I'm hoping, it's just good

So Where Was I?

I was always there, even if wasn't present
Actions louder than words, so still made me absent
No matter which way, to try mend the past
The damage was done, I can't undo that
What I'll prove, for the future I plea
To be there whenever, but can't guarantee
The lessons I've learnt, are hard ones to bear
So will try my upmost, your doubts be repaired
Forgiveness I ask, but do not expect
This apology shared, your right to reject

What's That Smell?

Purple and green mist, in the air
It lingers low, then creeps the stairs
Eyes now water and almost choke
It's suffocating, just like smoke
Faces screw up in disgust
As realise someone's done a puff
Giggles, as they find it funny
Denying, guessing, who it must be
Windows opened; freshener sprayed
Then it is obvious, who's to blame
'It must have been those naughty badgers'
Said Daddy, as adjusting trousers
Yes, no one else I know can parp
Or make a smell, like Daddy's fart

Treat

Really did I need do that?
Extravagant spend on dress and bag

It's for this year's posh Christmas party
So felt the need to be all sparkly

Feel guilty spending on myself
As should be buying for everyone else

Yes, hard it is to justify
The reasons why I had to buy

But this year has been awfully hard
And think I'm owed some small reward

Gorgeous, I will hopefully feel
From memories and pictures, forever yield

Is

So, it is? Depends what is?
Is, is someone, or something is?
I believe I'm often is
But on it's own, the is, is quizzed
Can't just be is, yet can just be
Like 'it' or 'so', not 'is', is see
Without the is, we do though miss
The glue, by other words exist
And is alone does not comply
Need is to make our reading right
So is he, is she, and is the World?
Or the World, she and he, an is?

New Lease of Life

I'm down in the dumps
As I sit here slumped
My belly rolled over my belt

Not always as felt
I used to be svelte
No worries for weight that I held

Blame having a baby
And no time just lately
To spend at the gym or to run

Instead of complaining
Efforts should be making
And thinking more of number one

Having spent too much time
Loving bad foods and wine
The effects are now on the outside

Determined I must
Be better and trust
That changes can reverse if tried

Once more fit my clothes
And energy grow
While skin and body then thrive

No longer feel stuffy
With bloated big tummy
No tight belt, but new lease of life

Springtime's Arrived

Marshmallow skies, pastels bounce off your eyes
Fluffy white clouds, with pink and blue stripes
First grass is cut, smells winter forgot
Flowers freshen the air, on trees and paths flock
Rain spits and spots, morning mist and due drops
Hearing birds joyfully singing, later into the clock
Warmer days and bright sunshine, tease of summer's born
Rainbows, thunder and hailstorms, show still must perform
Insects, bugs, butterflies, all buzzing by
Deer fill the fields, emerge from their hide
Spirits are lifted, such brightness inside
And so we all know, Springtime has arrived

Friday Nights

I cannot barely type these words
As tipple of two, or three, in turn
Ridiculous rhymes within my head
Are flooding out, too much is said

Oh silly me, how I forget
The limits wisely I had set
As now do stagger side to side
With wobbling strides, I cannot hide

Tomorrow might be a total mess
Headache and maybe some regrets
Did I say just what I thought
Oh no, look what the camera caught

But fun I had, good times are spent
With lovely friends at The King's Head
Memories made, and laughs we'll speak
Of Friday nights, when we all meet

Conveniences Etiquette

Please dispose in the right places
So not to leave unpleasant traces
Unfortunate for responsible ones
Who have no choice but to un-bung
Those behind may get a shock
If caused a flood, as you did block
Dirty not, so don't do wrong
And leave behind a nasty pong

Equality?

I agree women should be given rights
Equality with pay, chores spread alike

However, it seems it's all gone wrong
Still do my jobs, now more things along

A second wage earner, I work full time
I clean, tidy, cook to raise children fine

D.I.Y, dig garden and empty the bins
Taxi mum here and there, clubs brings

Washing, shopping, cleaning out pets
No time for hobbies, or looking my best

My fault to think, prove cope with all
Yet body not built for strength and toil

The stresses, strains, mind goes insane
And as a result, lifestyle's a pain

So being an equal isn't my case stronger
Give back my bra, want to live longer

Express Your Voice

Alone we sing, in car and bathroom
Not afraid, if song out of tune

Words might not be as they should
Yet every breath felt understood

If dare to open the windows out
And cry to others and shout aloud

Would the sound musically please
As birds in chorus, chirp and tweet

If the message comes across
Emotions of sadness, joy and love

Shared with every person passing
Notes to beckon, friendships lasting

Be brave, rejoice, you have a choice
Such gift you have, express your voice

Cheers

Let's celebrate, you hear us say
Keen to capture, and mark today
A drink or two, smiles and laughter
So, we remember, forever after

Acknowledgements

A special thanks goes out to my amazing editor and publisher Lorna Gray, for all her encouragement and help with realising my dream of getting my poems into a book. Also to Jeremy, for his fantastic artwork and for bringing my vision of the front cover to life.

I would like to thank all my wonderful family and friends for their love and support throughout my life. For allowing me to be myself and to believe that anything is possible if you try hard enough. Also, for giving me so many precious memories and hope for the future.

Dreams are the moments you have yet to create.
So put then in writing and discover your fate.